History

The goldfish, *Carassius auratus*, is the domesticated form of the wild Crucian carp, Genus *Carassius*, found in slow-moving waters in southern China. No one knows for certain when the process of domestication began, so conclusions are drawn from early Chinese art and literature. Based on this criterion, the goldfish is a modern pet compared to the domestication of dogs, cats, and even mice.

Chinese art features many examples of fish. However, the ornate nature of the products makes it difficult to identify the fish species. Colored fish are depicted on pottery dating from about 200 AD. Most authorities agree that the goldfish was developed later, from 800 AD onward. Selective breeding produced a number of color varieties by the time of the Sung Dynasty (circa 960-1379 AD). Interest quickened during the Ming Dynasty (1368–1643 AD). During that time, goldfish were first exported to Japan.

It is likely that the first

color mutations in carp appeared in stock farmed for food. Such novelties would have appealed to breeders. Hence, a trend developed toward improving such colors. As color mutations became well established, there was greater interest in retaining the best fish, both for further breeding and esthetic appreciation of the colors. Even greater interest was aroused as fin and eye mutations appeared.

It is generally believed that many of the basic modifications to the goldfish had been observed by the end of the Ming Dynasty. Further development of varieties moved from China to Japan, home of the famous koi carp, after 1650. The goldfish also became widespread in many other Far Eastern countries. Since Europeans were then developing strong trade links with the East, it was only a matter of time before goldfish journeyed to Europe.

They appeared in Europe during the 1700s and on American and Australian shores the following century. During these early years goldfish were kept in ponds. The hobby of keeping fish in tanks in the home did not become popular until the late 1800s.

DEVELOPMENT OF THE HOBBY

Over the years, fish of many kinds have been kept in various containers. Fishkeeping truly became popular with the public following the opening of the world's first aquarium in the London Zoo during 1853.

The relationship between fish, plants, and water had been observed by a medical surgeon, Ellis, as early as 1850, and by a chemist named Warrington. It was the naturalist Philip Henry Gosse, known as the father of fishkeeping, who put theory into practice.

Up to this time, it was considered impossible to keep marine life alive for more than a few days. Gosse built tanks to house marine fish and crustaceans. The water was aerated by syringes and replaced continually with salt water brought from the coast. Blinds were raised and lowered to regulate the amount of daylight allowed onto the tanks. Freshwater species soon were included in the display. The aquarium

CONTENTS

GOLDFISH
AS A NEW PET

ANMARIE BARRIE

1995 Edition

Published by T.F.H. Publications, Inc.
TFH Bldg., Neptune, NJ 07753, USA
Made in the USA

TU-001

Introduction

Klee's famous
painting entitled
GOLDFISH.

The common goldfish is the world's most popular pet. It is also the world's most abused pet. This latter situation is a result of the virtues that make the goldfish a good pet. It is a hardy species. It can adjust to and survive in conditions that kill most other species. These creatures are often confined in unsuitable containers with poor water quality. Because the goldfish survives for such a long time in such an appalling habitat, the owner surmises that the fish must be happy and healthy. However, the fact is that the fish just took a long time to die.

Fortunately, many goldfish owners understand the basic essentials of good fishkeeping. They know it is important to keep the water clean and well oxygenated and to choose a tank large enough to allow straight-line swimming. Their fish not only live longer, but also look healthier and are more pleasant to watch.

Modern technology has been utilized by tropical fish hobbyists. Coldwater

Klee's famous painting entitled GOLDFISH.

A side view of a Water Bubble-eye Goldfish

specialists also have benefited from the latest ideas in fishkeeping. Breeders have been improving the goldfish species and developing more varieties through selective breeding. Top exhibition fish are outstanding in their shape and color.

The singular advantage of goldfish over other species is that sophisticated equipment is not essential. Therefore, there are lower costs in setting up an aquarium and no risk that the system will be adversely affected by a power failure. The common goldfish is obtainable at a modest price. Even the fancier varieties are not expensive in comparison to other pets. The goldfish is an animal that requires little upkeep and minimal maintenance cost. It can be kept as a household pet or bred for exhibition. Aquarists are full of praise for the virtues of the goldfish.

was a huge success.

The public, having seen the possibilities of keeping fish in tanks, gathered all manner of waterlife. The majority of these creatures died due to ignorance concerning the importance of water conditions and feeding habits. Even the London Zoo closed its aquarium during the 1870s due to the difficulties of maintaining suitable conditions. However, the zoo set in motion the establishment of a hobby and of scientific research into the biology of water species.

Fish farms were common in many countries by the late 1800s. New varieties were being developed and old ones refined. The goldfish was a popular household pet throughout the world by the turn of the 20th century. The confined life of the goldfish became more humane as owners understood water chemistry and appreciated the need to maintain a biological equilibrium. Today there is no excuse for goldfish owners to subject their fish to anything but the finest living conditions due to our advanced technology and availablity of equipment.

The first goldfish show took place in Osaka, Japan as

early as 1862. In the West, there was a growing interest in forming animal societies as the 19th century drew to a close. Being a new, relatively easy and inexpensive hobby, keeping goldfish continued to grow through the 1920s. The first goldfish show in the West was probably organized by the British Aquarists Association in London in 1926. More shows followed as the hobby advanced.

Europeans took an interest in keeping goldfish in garden ponds following the Second World War. Previously this had been the preserve of the wealthy. The average man was able to feature an ornamental pond in his garden because of lower material costs. This aspect of goldfish keeping has continued to flourish.

THE FUTURE

The goldfish has managed to retain its popularity despite competition from other pets. Tropical fish are the main competitors of the goldfish. However, goldfish generally are less expensive. Advanced technology and new colors stimulate ongoing interest. Today's goldfish varieties are extremely attractive subjects in both tanks and ponds.

A closeup of the face of a Water Bubble-eye Goldfish.

Anatomy

Fishes are seen in a great assortment of shapes and sizes. Like other fishes, goldfish are well suited to their environment. Their shape reflects their need to move quickly and easily in water. These fish have a streamlined shape which produces a minimum amount of friction on its surface. Many fancy varieties no longer exhibit the original goldfish shape. However, this does not hinder them, provided they are kept within the safety of an aquarium.

SHAPE

The goldfish has an elongated oval shape. The body is slightly more convex on the dorsal surface. Viewed from the front, it is egg shaped, with the widest part about at the level of the eyes. The scales lie flat against the surface; they are covered with a mucus secretion which reduces friction and acts as a protective layer to the scales. This mucus gives a fish its slippery feel. A fish should be handled only with wet hands to prevent damage.

FINS

The goldfish has three single fins and two paired fins. Fins are used for propelling, stabilizing and braking.

The dorsal fin is large. It is about two-thirds of the body height at its apex and tapers sharply towards the tail. The fin contains about 20 fin rays composed of bone. The tallest are the first two or three. The dorsal fin acts rather like a keel to prevent rolling. It can be lowered for increased streamlining when the fish increases its speed. The fin is capable of rhythmic undulations when the fish remains motionless in the water. Varieties without a dorsal fin are less stable and less agile than the common goldfish.

Goldfish have the same organs as do most fishes, namely, a kidney, liver, and heart. They also have blood.

The caudal is also known as the tail fin. Its forked shape indicates the high speed capacity of these fish. The goldfish moves by a series of muscle contractions along its body—one side contracts as the other side relaxes. The fin rays of the tail can be moved from side to side to create maximum thrust.

the maneuvering movements of the fish. They can be raised or lowered, and operated in vertical or horizontal planes to give maximum flexibility.

The pectoral fins are found just behind the gill arches on the lower side of the fish. Their numerous functions include rapid turning, braking, and fanning for

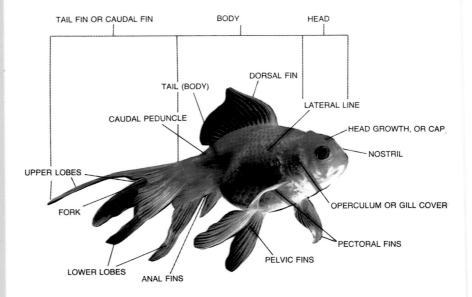

TAIL FIN OR CAUDAL FIN   BODY   HEAD

DORSAL FIN

TAIL (BODY)

LATERAL LINE

CAUDAL PEDUNCLE

HEAD GROWTH, OR CAP

NOSTRIL

UPPER LOBES

OPERCULUM OR GILL COVER

FORK

PECTORAL FINS

LOWER LOBES   ANAL FINS   PELVIC FINS

The anal fin is situated on the underside of the fish just forward of the caudal fin. It is used for stabilization.

The pelvic or ventral fins are located about mid-body, between the pectoral and anal fins. They are concerned principally with

stirring up the substrate.

A fish moves more slowly when the fins are modified to become paired and flowing. The muscles are not stronger in relation to the larger size, yet the fish has more surface area of fin to move. The extra size of the fin creates more friction, thus less speed.

THE HEAD

The head is the area to the front of the gills. It forms a continuous line into the body. The mouth is at the terminal end of the head. The position of the mouth of a fish gives a clue to its feeding habits. The mouth of the goldfish enables it to feed with ease at the surface, in midwater or on the bottom; thus it has not committed itself to feeding at a certain water level as have some fish species.

The goldfish has two pairs of nostrils just above the mouth. They are the organs of smell. They can detect both foods and pheromones (chemicals given off by fishes which relay messages). The fleshy parts of the nostrils are large in some goldfish, forming the pompoms for which that variety is named.

The eyes of a goldfish are large. Located on either side of the head, they give the fish monocular vision. This means that a fish cannot focus both eyes on a single image. Sight is good only in short ranges. The lack of eyelids gives a fish its apparent stare. Eyelids are unnecessary because the water itself acts as a lubricant.

Goldfish have a simple system of hearing. There is no outer ear because sound travels better in the relatively dense medium of water than in air; hence, no funneling mechanism is required. The ears of the fish are connected to the swim bladder, so they

A beautiful pair of Calico Telescope-eyed Goldfish.

aid in balance as well as hearing. A fish is likely to have difficulty in maintaining its swimming position if its hearing apparatus is damaged.

11

LATERAL LINE

Along the center of a fish's body, extending to its mouth, is a series of modified scales called the lateral line. These scales are sensitive to vibrations in the water. They are connected to each other by a mucus-filled channel. The lateral line complements the other senses by alerting a fish to the slightest changes in the water current.

SWIMBLADDER

The swimbladder, also known as air-sacs, is beneath the backbone of most fish species. It is a modification to the alimentary tract. This bladder is made up of two compartments containing oxygen, carbon dioxide, and nitrogen. The fish rises or descends in the water by deflating or inflating the air-sacs. The swimbladder may be adversely affected when a fish is bred to an unnatural shape. The result is a tendency towards instability and abnormal swimming positions.

SCALES

The body of a fish is covered with a series of transparent scales. There are no scales on the head, which is itself a bony plate structure. The scales form early in life; their number remains constant throughout the life of the fish. The outer edges of the scales grow as the fish grows. No new scales appear other than to replace any that might be damaged.

A trained eye can detect the extent of growth in a goldfish. This is because the rate of growth varies according to the season and general conditions of feeding. Growth rings on the scales appear at the end of each season. Thus the rings will be close together in poor years, indicating little growth.

The skin of a fish is composed of an outer layer, the epidermis, and a thicker inner layer, the dermis. The scales are embedded in the dermis. Within the dermis are blood vessels and a light-reflecting substance known as guanine. Guanine is found in all living tissues; it is part of the chemical make-up of the cell nucleus. The reflective layer gives the body of a fish its metallic shine. It reflects light, as well as the pigment colors present in the dermis and epidermis, back to the viewer.

Color pigment in fish is comprised of the red-yellow lipochromes and the black melanin. These are found within cells called chromatophores. The shape of these cells is governed by various factors, one of which is hormone action. Thus a fish can modify its color according to mood. Other factors, such as feeding, environmental temperatures, mutations, and the state of the water, also determine color. Since colors are the result of complex chemical actions and combinations, anything that alters the chemical make-up of a cell affects the color.

Gene action has affected goldfish in two ways. First, it increases or decreases the density of color. For example, diluted black becomes brown and then blue. Other pigments show similar changes. Secondly, the reflective layer of tissue may be reduced or absent. When this happens, pigments deeper in the

dermis are visible. Breeders classify goldfish according to scale type. Actually, this is a bit misleading because there is no difference in the scales per se, but in the reflective layer. Maybe "reflective" type would be a more appropriate term.

Metallic types have the reflective tissue intact. These fishes have a high gloss appearance. Such fish may be red-orange or shades of yellow. They can be black, greenish-brown or silver.

Nacreous types have a pearl-like sheen to them. This muted reflection is caused by a reduction in the

If you look closely at the scales on this Ryukin, they almost look like a series of dominos, one overlapping the other.

13

thickness of the reflective tissue. Since more pigment is visible, the potential color range is increased to include pink, brown, blue, and black. These colors may occur in combination to create the pattern referred to as calico.

Matte types have no reflective tissue. The result is a flat or matte appearance. The potential range of colors is similar to the nacreous types.

It is possible for a goldfish to exhibit two types of reflective colors on different areas of the body. It is better, though, for a fish to be purely one of the three basic types.

RESPIRATION

Fish require oxygen just as mammals do. A fish's oxygen is obtained directly from the water. This calls for a different method of processing oxygen than that utilized by air-breathing animals.

Fish take in water through the mouth. The water is passed over a complex system of filaments on the inner side of the gills. These filaments are rich in blood vessels. The oxygen is filtered from the water to be passed in to the circulatory system of the fish. The water, carbon dioxide, and ammonia are passed out through the gills.

Knowing that the fish get their oxygen from the water is of considerable importance. If fish are taking dissolved oxygen from the water, then a given volume of water can support only a certain number of fish. The fish will have difficulty breathing if the water is overstocked. They will gasp for air at the surface because the greatest concentration of dissolved oxygen is there.

There are some important points to remember concerning the amount of oxygen in the water. First, as the water temperature increases, the amount of oxygen in the water decreases. Second, the surface area of the tank or pond has a direct bearing on the oxygen level. The greater the surface area per given volume of water, the more dissolved oxygen it contains. Third, aeration can increase the oxygen content. The more the water is circulated to the top, the more opportunity it has to pick up oxygen from the air.

BODY TEMPERATURE

Fish are poikilothermic, or cold-blooded. This does not mean that fish have cold blood. Rather, their blood temperature is not constant but is governed by their environment. Some fish can survive only within limited temperature ranges. Others, the goldfish included, can withstand wide fluctuations.

DIGESTION

Goldfish are omnivorous feeders—they require vegetable and protein matter in their diet. Because they can cope with plant cellulose, their digestive tract is longer than that of carnivorous (meat-eating) animals. This is because plant material is more difficult than animal matter to break down into its component parts. Protein is more easily digested than cellulose, but it is more difficult to obtain. This explains why meats and livefoods are more expensive by weight than their plant food equivalents.

Goldfish do not have teeth. They crush food by pharyngeal "teeth" at the back of the mouth. Food passes from here into the gullet. In the stomach, enzyme action breaks it down into a paste-like consistency. This process continues in the intestines; by this time, the food is a liquid. Nutrients are absorbed through the intestinal wall into the bloodstream. Waste products advance to the alimentary canal to be excreted as feces via the anus. The goldfish

A rare White Matt-scaled Bubble-eye. The matt scaling makes the fish look scaleless.

has a liver, kidney and other organs which aid in digestion.

The concentration of a freshwater fish's blood is greater than that of the surrounding water. This means that goldfish must expel large quantities of water continuously via the gills and as urine via the anus.

REPRODUCTIVE ORGANS

The male reproductive organs are known as testes. Those of the female are called ovaries. The reproductive organs of both sexes are located just below the swimbladder; eggs and sperm exit via gonopores. (The gonad is the tissue in which the reproductive organs develop.) Goldfish are non-dimorphic. This means that the sexes look alike. Only at breeding time can the sexes be distinguished.

A magnificent Ryukin Goldfish.

The Aquatic Ecosystem

The main objective of an aquarist is to create a balanced aquatic environment within a given volume of water. The living and non-living components must form an attractive display, be maintained with a minimum of effort, and afford the fish a stress-free life. In an aquarium, it is important to be sure that no one component of the system dominates the environment. Very little needs to go wrong in a confined aquarium to induce a negative cycle.

Of course, we cannot really duplicate a natural habitat in a pond or aquarium. Nor should we attempt to. Wild habitats present a multitude of undesirable elements, such as predatory fish, temperature fluctuations and chemical saturation. Nonetheless, natural processes should be utilized wherever possible in an artificial environment.

THE LIFE CYCLE

Water in a wild habitat is constantly on the move. Thus it does not lose its condition as does standing water. The cycle begins as rainwater falling on the mountains. As the water flows, it collects both soluble and insoluble chemicals which affect its quality. For example, if the water courses over chalky rocks, it becomes hard and alkaline due to the presence of the dissolved minerals. If the water runs over granite, it becomes soft and acid because less minerals are dissolved. These conditions can be measured.

Because of its constant movement, the water moves debris downstream. Undesirable chemicals do not build up, thus the ratio of the chemicals to the volume of water is fairly stable. Decaying matter is also swept downstream. Dead plants and animals do not represent an appreciable mass in relation to the water volume.

Additionally, anaerobic bacteria convert dead material into a variety of compounds, the most important of which is ammonia. Excess ammonia is toxic to fish and plant life.

However, in moving water it is present only in dilute form. Furthermore, aerobic bacteria convert ammonia and other dangerous chemicals into nitrites and nitrates. Nitrogen, a by-product of this conversion, is harmless to the water organisms and eventually dissipates into the atmosphere.

The nitrites, nitrates, and other minerals are absorbed by plants as part of their food intake. Additionally, minerals are absorbed by the fish. Although the plant life is eaten by fish and other animals, the animal population rarely exceeds the food supply.

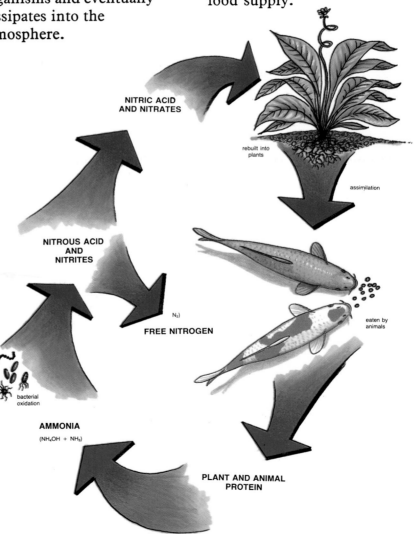

NITRIC ACID AND NITRATES

rebuilt into plants

assimilation

NITROUS ACID AND NITRITES

N₂)

FREE NITROGEN

eaten by animals

bacterial oxidation

AMMONIA

(NH₄OH + NH₃)

PLANT AND ANIMAL PROTEIN

During the day, plants respire by a process known as photosynthesis. They release oxygen into the water and absorb carbon dioxide. At night the process is reversed as they take in oxygen. Fish take in less oxygen at night, though, when they tend to have longer rest periods. There is typically a surplus of oxygen over the entire 24-hour cycle.

Life in a river changes as the seasons change. Plants die and the fish are less active as winter approaches. Plants lower on the evolutionary scale, such as algae and simple free-floating species, are more apparent. The fish survive mainly on fat reserves as the river remains in a dormant state. They seek refuge in deeper, warmer water where they are less readily seen by predators.

The simpler plants utilize the sun's rays and multiply rapidly as spring advances. Slow-moving rivers and ponds display the well-recognized blanket of algal growth. The free-swimming life forms containing chlorophyll also multiply, so the water becomes cloudy or green.

More advanced plant life reaches the middle and higher water levels as summer comes. The water clears as the algae is prevented from obtaining nutrients and sunshine. The increasing activity of the fish and other water creatures also takes its toll on the algal plants.

The ebb and flow of the life cycle retains its delicate balance throughout the year. No one plant, chemical or animal enjoys more than a brief period of domination before changes in the water neutralize matters. No doubt you can appreciate how easily such an ecosystem can be upset or destroyed.

THE NEGATIVE CYCLE

The pace of a river slows as it moves over flat lands. The rain is polluted by the chemical discharge in the air from factories. These contaminants are added to the chemicals already present in the water. Dust settles on the quieter reaches of the waterway. This filters the sunlight and reduces the oxygen exchange at the water surface.

Anaerobic bacteria, not

needing oxygen, multiply to the point where they release more harmful chemicals than can be converted by the aerobic bacteria. Soon black sludge covers the rocks. The beneficial bacteria die out in increasing numbers. The plants die due to the shortage of nitrites and nitrates and the increase of chemicals. The algal growth becomes more rampant, which in turn reduces the light available to the plants. More decaying matter is created.

Both fish and other organisms suffer as a result of the lack of vegetation and the increase in ammonium compounds. Only the hardiest of plant species survive. The growth of the fish is stunted and reproductive vigor fails. Eventually there are no fish of certain species.

AVOIDING PROBLEMS

It is not possible to avoid all problems in an aquarium. However, the risk can be reduced to an acceptable level. Steps can be taken to counter potential hazards because we know about the cycles of life in water. Periodic tests need to be done to examine and correct the chemical state of the water. There are some key points to bear in mind.

1. The aquarium structure itself should be as large as possible. This slows the rapid changes in the condition of the water.
2. Circulate the water and have some turbulence at its surface. This ensures a constant temperature throughout its depth and maintains an adequate oxygen supply. However, movement of the water should not be so rapid that it affects plant growth.
3. Provide a filtration system to remove unwanted debris and harmful chemicals.
4. Add only clean water to the tank. The water must not contain unwanted organisms or dissolved chemicals.
5. The plant selection should reflect the temperature of the water. Include only those plants which thrive in the temperature range of your tank.
6. Maintain the water temperature within

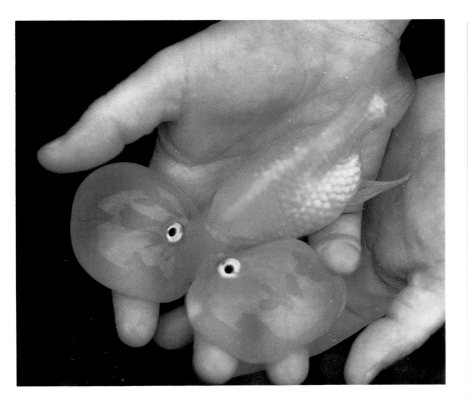

acceptable variables. Avoid sudden temperature fluctuations.

7. Illuminate the aquarium to equate a natural day-night cycle.

8. Do not overfeed the goldfish. Excess food sinks to the substrate, where it decomposes and helps foul the tank.

9. Treat ill fish in an isolation tank. The spread of disease must be restricted.

10. Subject any addition to the aquarium, whether living or not, to careful scrutiny. Toxic chemicals, parasites, and bacterial infections must not be introduced.

makes practical sense because a larger unit is easier to maintain than a smaller one. In addition, a really attractive exhibit can be displayed in a large tank—one that would not be possible in a small tank. The number of goldfish that can be contained in an aquarium is greatly influenced by the size and shape of the aquarium.

SIZE AND SHAPE

Surface area is the most important measurement of an aquarium. This determines how much oxygen can be dissolved within a given volume of water. This, in turn, controls the stock levels.

Two containers may hold the same volume of water yet have different surface areas. Thus the shape of a tank is an important factor. A unit 60 by 30 cm (24 by 12 in) has a surface area of 1800 sq cm (288 sq in). The surface area will not be altered no matter how high such a unit is. Hence, an aquarium with a depth of 90 cm (36 in) cannot accommodate any more fish than a unit 30 cm (12 in) deep. The deeper unit merely provides more

The Aquarium

A complete ecosystem must be developed within the aquarium unit. As far as the fish are concerned, the aquarium is their entire world, so the unit should be as large as possible for the fish to thrive in it. This also swimming space. The amount of oxygen in the lower depths is restricted, however, so the fish will probably not swim there.

Surface area controlled the shape of tanks for many years. The standard rectangle remained the most popular shape for practical reasons. It has a good surface area and provides for maximum viewing of the fish. Nowadays, round, octagonal and even triangular aquariums are available. This is because the oxygen level can be increased by artificial means.

Most aquarium tanks are rectangular, but other shapes are represented as well. The amount of surface area of the water is a more important consideration than shape alone— although in almost every case a bowl-shaped receptacle is much less desirable than an aquarium. Photo courtesy of California Aquarium Supply Co.

MATERIALS

Aquariums are made of acrylic or glass. Acrylics vary in quality from inexpensive small bowls to better compounds used in larger aquariums. The quality is reflected in the price— lowcost units tend to scratch more easily and yellow with age. Small goldfish bowls and tanks have no merits for use as permanent fish homes. They are suited only for use as spare containers for isolating or breeding fish.

The better acrylics of large aquariums have good clarity and are scratch-resistant.

Glass is still the favored material, however. It cleans readily, provides maximum clarity, lasts for years, and is competitively priced.

Rubber silicon bondings have replaced ugly metal frames. This material has permitted new design possibilities. Some enthusiasts make their own aquariums to meet specific requirements. If you do purchase a metal-framed aquarium, check it carefully for leaks and erosion.

STOCKING LEVELS

You must estimate the number of goldfish that can be housed in your aquarium before stocking. Do not exceed this number or the health of your fish will be endangered. The standard basis of calculation for a tank without mechanical aeration is 155 square centimeters of surface area for every 2.5 cm of body length of fish, excluding the tail. This is 24 square inches for every one inch of body length, excluding the tail. For example, a tank measuring 60 by 30 cm is calculated as follows: $60 \times 30 = 1800 \div 155$ square centimeters $= 11.6 \times 2.5$ cm $= 29$ cm (11.4 in) total possible body length.

Divide the total potential body length by the average size of the fully grown fish you want to keep. This figure tells you how many goldfish can be kept safely in the tank. For instance, if you want to keep fish averaging 5 cm (2 in) in length in a tank with the total possible body length of 29 cm (11.4 in), then divide 5 cm (4 in) into 29 cm (11.4). The result is that five to six of this size fish can be kept comfortably in the tank. This may not seem like a large number, but this stocking level ensures an adequate oxygen supply to each fish in a tank without mechanical aeration.

Bear in mind that the addition of an airstone increases the fish capacity of a tank. Another point to remember is that warmer water holds less oxygen, so it is not wise to keep a lot of fish unless auxiliary equipment is used.

POTENTIAL SIZE OF GOLDFISH

The potential size of a goldfish is influenced by a number of factors. Average sizes are dependent on the permutations of these growth variables.

Each goldfish is born with a genetic potential for its growth. All other things being equal, some fish will be bigger than others. However, "all other things" are *not* equal. The rate of growth is influenced by both temperature and food quality. Within the confines of a tank, the temperature is reasonably stable. Therefore, diet is a more critical factor. Additionally, goldfish have hormonal inhibitors that

24

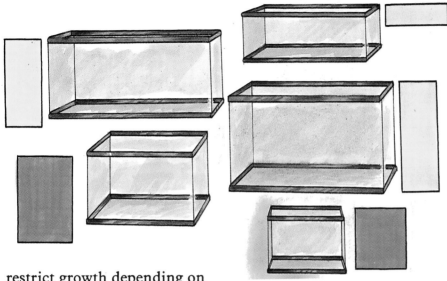

restrict growth depending on available space. Fish in small tanks will not attain the size they could have in larger aquariums.

AQUARIUM WEIGHT

The total weight of a small aquarium is not usually a problem. The situation changes dramatically as the overall dimensions of the tank increase. The heaviest component is the water. Combined with substrate gravel, rocks, equipment, fish, and the tank unit, a substantial weight is created. This is important to consider when siting the aquarium.

A shelf is a risky site for a tank. A stand must have strong supports and be even to prevent a tank from going over. Wooden floors often seem solid, but they are certainly tested by a large tank. You may opt to build a sturdy base of brick for a very big aquarium. Just be sure that whatever site you choose for your aquarium can adequately support the heavy weight.

As an example of weight calculation, consider a tank 90 by 38 by 30 cm (36 by 15 by 12 in). The glass weighs about 1.47 kg per 0.093 square meter (3¼ lb per square foot) at 10 mm (⅜ in) thickness. The water weighs one kg per liter (10 lb per Imp gal/8.345 lb per US gal). Medium-sized gravel, 5 cm (2 in) deep, spreads at a rate approximately one kg to every 863 cc (1 lb to 24 cubic inch). The total is 17.6 kg glass + 103 kg water + 19.58 kg gravel = 140.18 kg (39.8 + 234 + 45 = 318.8 lb). This weight does not even account for the equipment, plants or fish. This gives you an idea of how deceptively heavy an aquarium is in relation to its size.

as feeding and maintenance are made easier. The canopy should incorporate a number of ventilation holes so that carbon dioxide and heat can escape.

Typical lighting uses either tungsten filament bulbs or fluorescent tubes. Sometimes both are featured. Tungsten lamps are inexpensive and easily fitted into canopies or hoods. They produce a light

LIGHTING

Lighting has two functions: illumination and plant growth. Lighting is usually housed in a canopy or hood. Metal canopies are heavy, so many are made from plastic.

Canopies with hinged lids are superior to those that need to be raised completely,

that is adequate for the propagation of plants. It is possible to purchase them in a range of watts without any increase in the size of the bulb. A drawback for coldwater aquarists is that the lamps produce a lot of heat. They are also more costly to run than tube lights, have a shorter life and were designed for pendant fitting rather than horizontal use.

Fit a protective sleeve over the connector (where they plug in) and use plastic rather than metal fittings. To calculate the amount of wattage necessary, multiply the length of the tank in inches by 3.25. Thus a 48 inch aquarium needs 48 × 3.25 or 156 watts of

illuminaton. This can be supplied by three 60-watt or four 40-watt bulbs.

Fluorescent tubes are more costly to install and more difficult to fit than tungsten bulbs, but they are cheaper to run. Some tubes require starter motors and chokes, which are heavy items. Other tubes have automatic

transformers in a single box which can be placed within the hood or mounted nearby.

Fluorescent lighting gives an even spread of light which is generated on low power. It also has a low heat output. The tubes are less likely than tungsten bulbs to shatter if splashed with water. Fluorescent tubes come in many forms. Some equate natural daylight; others have increased color effects within the natural spectrum. Tubes are also more beneficial for plant growth. However, they are more restricted in wattage-to-size ratios.

The standard method to calculate the wattage needed for fluorescent tubes is 10 watts for every 30 cm (12 in) of tank length. For example, a 120-cm (48 in) unit requires 40 watts of lighting.

Whether using tungsten or fluorescent lights, the calculations do not take into account the tank width. Since tanks come in such an assortment of widths these days, assume the calculations are based on a 30-cm (12 in) wide tank. Increase the calculated wattage accordingly. A 120 by 60 cm (48 by 24 in) unit requires 80 watts of fluorescent lighting, while a tank of the same length but only 45 cm (18 in) wide requires 60 watts.

Position bulbs or tubes to avoid shadows. Place them toward the front and rear of the tank if two are used, or near the front if only one is fitted. Some aquarists utilize shadows and darker areas as part of the overall scene to achieve a dramatic effect.

A number of other factors affect the amount of light that falls onto a given area. Dust on the tubes, condensation and dust on the cover plate, and dust on the water surface reduce the intensity of the light.

DURATION OF LIGHT

Plants need about 12 hours of light a day. Adjustments can be made depending on the state of the aquarium. Once the plants have received sufficient light, the excess is used by green algae. Reduce the intensity or duration of the light if the green algae becomes rampant, or, increase the number of plants in the tank. Since different plants require different intensity and exposure, a satisfactory balance between the living organisms will probably be achieved only by trial and error.

NATURAL SUNLIGHT

You may want to place the aquarium in a sunny spot to get the necessary light. There are some problems with this approach, though. Plants and fish are phototropic. This means that they respond to the direction of the light and grow towards it.

Under the natural conditions in a river, light enters from above, so the plants grow upward. Having natural sunlight enter from above is rarely possible in a home setting. Rather, the sunlight usually enters from the sides. Plants will lean sideways instead of growing straight up. Fish may lean over or swim at an angle.

These situations are not desirable in an aquarium.

Another drawback is that the duration of natural light is variable from day to day. It can range from many hours to practically nothing. Algae will soon cover the substrate, rocks, and glass if there is too much light. Brown algae flourishes when a tank is underlit.

An aquarium can easily be lit by high intensity light fixtures suspended over them. This allows for bog plants to grow out of the tank and for the room to be humidified from the evaporating water. High intensity lights can be ordered through most aquarium shops.

Daylight also fluctuates in its intensity. Therefore, the temperature of the water can be altered much too widely for the good of the fish and the plant life. These unstable conditions create too many problems in a restricted volume of water. These aspects can be controlled to provide a more natural environment by using artificial light.

LIGHT CHANGES

Fish do not adapt to sudden changes in the intensity of light. They are less able than we are to shield their eyes from brightness. This is why a dimmer switch should be considered. The dimmer can be controlled by a timer. The brightness is gradually reduced as the light is turned off. The reverse happens as the light is turned on. If you do not opt for a dimmer switch, turn on a room light before lighting up the aquarium to give the fish a chance to adjust.

WATER

Water is the single most important component in an aquarium. Its condition determines whether or not

Fluorescent tubes for aquarium lighting fixtures come in a number of different wattages and light spectra—and of course some are much longer than others. Pet dealers can provide sensible advice about lighting choices. Photo courtesy of Hagen.

Aquarium thermometers are available in a few different basic types; shown is a digital type that can be attached to the side of the aquarium. Photo courtesy of Hagen.

the container will support life. The quality, composition, and temperature of the water must be correct for the particular species of fish kept. Dirt and toxic chemicals must be removed from the water, and an adequate supply of oxygen must be available at all times.

Water is graded according to its properties. It can be hard or soft, acid or alkaline, and fresh or salt. The nitrite content can be determined as well.

Aquarists classify fish either as saltwater or freshwater based on their required water types. These two groups are further divided into tropical or coldwater species, depending on their temperature range. Plants are described by these same criteria. From them a fishkeeper can determine whether or not a given species of fish or plant can survive within the water of his aquarium.

The basic requirements of goldfish can be summarized as follows. They are freshwater, coldwater fish. They can tolerate degrees of hardness, but extremes should be avoided. Goldfish prefer a pH that is neutral to slightly acid or alkaline. A range of 6.5 to 8.5 is acceptable. The free nitrogen in the water should be less than one mg per liter. This is equal to 3.3 mg of nitrite. The lower the nitrogen level, the lower the nitrite content. A good reading is below 0.5 mg. Temperatures of 12.7–18.3°C (55–65°F) are favored. Goldfish can survive in temperature ranges of 1.7–35°C (35–95°F). Exotic varieties in particular should be protected from temperature extremes.

Hardness: The more dissolved salts in the water, the harder it is; the less dissolved salts, the softer the water. Hardness may be viewed in two ways. First, there is total or general hardness. Second, there is temporary hardness. The latter is a result of carbonates of calcium or magnesium present in the water.

Hardness is measured by three methods. These are calculated in degrees, either English, German or American. The English degree is based on the amount of calcium carbonate

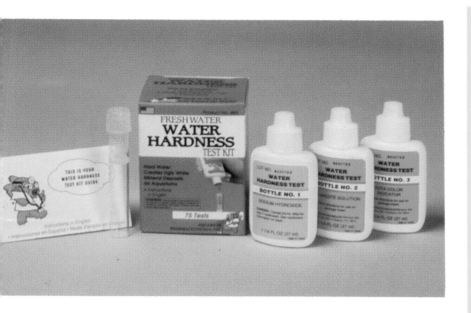

The hardness of the water in which they are maintained can be an important consideration in the health of goldfsh; test kits for measuring water hardness are easy to use and widely available. Photo courtesy of Aquarium Pharmaceuticals.

(CaCO₃) in each Imperial gallon; the German degree on the amount of calcium oxide (CaO) in 100 k parts of water; while the American degree represents the number of grains of calcium carbonate per one million parts of water (ppm). Multiplying the English degree by 14.3 and the German degree by 17.9 yields the measurement in parts per million. This is a convenient unit of measurement.

The ideal water hardness for goldfish ranges from 125–268 ppm. This is slightly to moderately hard. Hardness may be reduced in a number of ways. There are four popular options:

1. Boiling the water to remove temporary hardness. The cooled water is mixed with the tank water to dilute the overall hardness. This is impractical for large volumes.

2. Collecting rainwater to dilute the tank water. By testing the rainwater and the water of the tank, the hardness of the mix can be calculated. Assume the rainwater has 60 ppm and the tank water 400 ppm. If you

exchange 40 liters of a 100-liter tank, you have 60 liters at 400 ppm and 40 at 60 ppm. The mix reads $60 \times 400 + 40 \times 60 = 264$ ppm in the aquarium.

3. Adding hydrogen resins to convert the calcium carbonate into carbonic acid and calcium resin. The carbonic acid refers to water and carbon dioxide.
4. Using peat in the filter. The peat absorbs the calcium to soften the water.

pH: The pH is determined by the number of hydrogen ions in the water. This is expressed on a logarithmic index of 0–14. The water is neutral at a reading of 7. Below 7 is acidic, above is alkaline. A movement of one degree represents a change in pH of ten times the previous state. Water of 6 on the scale is ten times more acidic than water of 5, and 100 times more acidic than a reading of 4.

Test kits can be purchased from your dealer. Typically, some test liquid is added to a sample of tank water. The water changes color and is compared against a color chart or disc. Some tests utilize litmus red: red indicates acid, blue is alkaline. Another option is to dip the terminals of a pH meter into the water. Adjusting the pH is not difficult. However, sudden changes of pH stress a goldfish, so care must be exercised when altering the pH level. When changing or adding water to the tank, be sure that the pH is not radically affected.

Add limestone or chalk chips to raise the pH value. Sodium carbonate makes the water harder, however, so add sodium carbonate to counter the effect. (You may have noticed by now that pH and hardness or softness are linked. Hard water tends to be alkaline, while soft waters are usually acidic). Acidity is often the result of an incomplete breakdown of waste products. Check the filters and the substrate gravel; they may be blocked or need to be replaced. Add peat to the filter to lower the pH value. Whether raising or lowering the pH, change the water gradually over a few days. Use water of the pH value that you are trying to maintain in the tank.

Since 1952, Tropical Fish Hobbyist has been the source of accurate, up-to-the-minute, and fascinating information on every facet of the aquarium hobby. Join the many thousands of devoted readers worldwide who wouldn't miss a single issue.

Reptile Hobbyist is the source for accurate, up-to-the-minute, practical information on *every* facet of the herpetological hobby. Join many thousands of devoted readers worldwide who wouldn't miss a single valuable issue.

Subscribe right now so you don't miss a single copy!

Copper: Excess copper in the water can kill the fish. If you have copper pipes in your home, run some water through your tap before using it in the aquarium. This is particularly important if the water has been standing in the pipes for some time; the concentration of copper in the water will be even higher than normal.

Chlorine: Most city water authorities add chlorine to tapwater as a sterilizing measure. This is good for us, but not for our fish. Before introducing water into the tank, allow it to stand for 24 hours. The chlorine will evaporate into the air. This process can be sped up by agitating the water periodically.

Water Changing: About 20–25% of the tank water should be changed every two to four weeks. The time interval depends on the size of the aquarium and how well its systems are functioning. Try your best to equate the components of the fresh water, such as hardness, pH and temperature, with those of the tank in order to lessen the stress on the fish. When emptying the tank, siphon from the lower levels to remove debris on the substrate.

Goldfish keepers can buy kits that allow maintenance of the water in an aquarium at a particular pH level. The four kits shown here, for example, would allow a range from relatively weakly acidic through strongly (by aquarium water standards, anyway) alkaline. Photo courtesy of Aquarium Pharmaceuticals.

Aeration and Filtration

AERATION

The amount of water surface dictates how much oxygen the water will contain. This, in turn, determines how many fish can be kept. When the water is flat, such as in a non-mechanically aerated tank, the surface maximum is that of the container. By increasing the surface area dimensions or by agitating the water of the smaller container, the rate of exchange of oxygen can be increased.

To fully appreciate this point, consider that a straight line runs between two sides of the aquarium. If the water is flat, the line will be flat. Now picture that same line resting on top of wavy water. The length of the line must increase in proportion to the size of the waves because the agitated water has a greater surface area than flat water. This is the effect of mechanical aeration. The reason that many goldfish survive in unaerated tanks is simply because the tank is not overstocked. If the number of fish were increased, they would spend more time near the surface—a sure sign that the water lacks oxygen.

Mechanical aeration also has another benefit in addition to increasing surface area. Because it creates currents, the temperature of the water remains more constant throughout the depth of the tank than if the water were static.

Aeration can be achieved simply by attaching a piece of plastic tubing to a small pump. The air outlet end of the tube is positioned near the base of the tank. The rising air bubbles create a current that circulates the water. The bubbles burst as they reach the surface. The miniature waves formed agitate the water surface. It is not really the air bubbles that oxygenate the water; it is the turbulence at the surface.

Pumps are available in many sizes and power output levels. The power is measured in flow rates of liters or gallons per hour. There are some factors that you should consider when purchasing a pump. For instance, be sure that spare

parts are readily obtainable. Don't buy a pump that is very noisy when in operation; the better models are the quieter ones. In addition, the pump should have an adjustable output.

You may use the pump solely to supply air to the aquarium. A small capacity model serves this purpose. However, if the pump is to supply air to a filter system, a more powerful model is in order. It is always a good idea to acquire a pump that works easily within its capacity rather than one which must operate at peak performance.

The diaphragm or vibrator pump is popular. It is a bit noisy, but it is better and easier to use than many other pumps. It can be suspended in order to reduce the noise. Do not cover the pump, however, or the unit will overheat.

When siting a pump less than 30 cm (12 in) above a tank, fit a non-return valve to the air outlet pipe. This prevents water from being siphoned into the system when the pump is turned off. If water gets into the pump, there could be damage and flooding.

Aeration can be made into

an attractive feature of the tank. Diffuser stones can be used to form a wall of tiny bubbles at the back of the aquarium. The smaller bubbles discharged from airstones are more likely to burst in midwater. This is beneficial because oxygen is released directly into the water.

FILTRATION

Filtration is the removal of unwanted chemicals and debris from the water. The aquarium stays clean, clear, and healthy. Ideally, water should be drawn from the bottom of the tank, where it is the dirtiest and least oxygenated. The flow rate of a filtration system should

circulate about twice the water capacity of the aquarium per hour. There are three basic methods of filtration. One or a combination may be used in a tank.

Mechanical filtration passes the water through one or a number of filter mediums. The debris is trapped, but the water passes back into the tank. The fineness of the medium determines the degree of filtration. Common filter media are wool and activated charcoal. Charcoal is actually a double filter; it strains debris from the water as well as combining chemically with minerals to create inert compounds.

Chemical filtration removes chemicals from the water that normally pass through a mechanical filter. The chemicals pass through mechanical filters because they are either in solution or so small that they cannot be strained out of the water. Filters, such as charcoal and zeolite, convert chemicals into less harmful products.

Biological filtration does not actually remove anything from the water. Toxic products are converted into other compounds to be used by plants. The residue dissipates into the atmosphere.

FILTER SYSTEMS

Units may be located in or out of the aquarium. They may be air-lift or powered units. The latter are more beneficial for large volumes of water or where maximum clarity is desired.

Air-lift filters have an air tube positioned in a wider tube. The wider tube is inserted into a plastic box containing a number of holes. The uppermost opening exits outside the box. The box is packed with nylon wool or a similar filter material. Air leaving the narrow tube rises in the larger tube. In doing so, water is drawn through the filter to exit via the top opening. This water is replaced by water drawn into the filter through the holes in the filter box. The drawing power of an air-lift filter is limited to the area immediately around it. It is used only in small tanks.

External box filters are more popular. These are hung on the side or back of the aquarium. Water is siphoned through a tube and discharged into the filter box. Air is passed through a tube into the bottom of the filter unit. This tube enters a larger one. The air and water are returned to the tank above the water surface. The filter unit may contain a medium such as nylon wool, activated charcoal, gravel chips or sand.

Power filters are the better choice for large aquariums. No air pump is needed and the volume of filtered water is greater. Essentially, water is pumped through the filter unit and returned to the tank surface by a single tube or a spray bar. A spray bar has small holes along its length to provide maximum agitation to the water surface. It is unnecessary to have a separate supply of air for aeration when using a power filter since aeration occurs as the water is returned to the tank from the filter.

A power filter may be an internal or external canister. In addition, the filter may be an external box type, resembling an air-lift filter. Choose a model with a flow capacity to suit your tank size. A filter too powerful for your system may have an adverse affect on plant growth due to its strong currents.

Undergravel filters are the best biological filters. Air is sent down a tube to rise within a larger tube. This tube is attached to a corrugated plate on the base of the tank. The plate should cover at least two-thirds, if not all, of the tank floor.

Eventually the base filter plate becomes populated with aerobic bacteria. As water passes down from the substrate gravel, the bacteria convert ammonium compounds to nitrates. The water is drawn into the air-lift tube and returned via an outlet at the water surface. The water is sprayed onto the surface as fine jets. The harmless nitrates are used by the plants as nutrients. Instead of raising the water via an air-lift, the process can be speeded up by fitting a power head to the outlet to suck up the water.

Because an undergravel filter is at the base of the aquarium, it must be installed when the tank is initially set up. It takes some time for the system to become fully operational since the beneficial bacteria

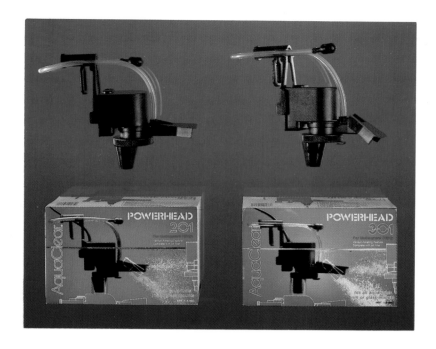

need to colonize and mature on the filter plate and gravel. You may wish to embed some plastic mesh deep in the gravel. This prevents exposure of the filter plate as the goldfish forage in the substrate.

The currents created by undergravel filters disturb some plants. It may be necessary to relocate the plants in order for them to find a suitable spot.

Reverse flow filters are more complex. As the name suggests, the water movement is the reverse of the normal situation. An external filter draws water from the base of the tank, just above the gravel, and into the filter. The filtered water is directed into the undergravel air tube and below the filter plate. The water then rises through the plate and through the gravel. The advantage of this system is that only clean water passes through the filter and gravel. The disadvantage is that the water is less aerated than in conventional systems.

Aquascaping

Aquascaping is the development of a three-dimensional "picture" within the confines of an aquarium. The most popular approach to aquascaping is creating a scene that imparts to the layman the concept of a natural habitat. In reality, the scenes are usually far from realistic. The variety of props is broad—plants, rocks, wood, gravel, and plastic ornaments.

The beneficial properties of living plants and real rocks should not be overlooked. They help create conditions in the water essential to fish. A fish aquarist will not dismiss artificial decorations, however. Used with care and artistic positioning, they have a number of advantages. For instance, a plastic boulder which weighs substantially less than its real counterpart may be more practical in a large aquarium. An imitation tree branch can hide equipment piping or an internal filter. Plastic plants can be substituted for delicate plants that may not survive the attention of goldfish.

PLANNING

The siting of the aquarium affects the planning of the aquascene. Some aquariums can only be viewed from the front. Others can be approached from the sides as well. The internal layout of the tank must be developed with this in mind.

You must pre-plan the scene so you know what materials and decorations are required. A rough sketch is suitable. Here you can indicate the placement of rocks, terracing, and filter tubes. In positioning plants, place at the back those that attain the greatest heights. Some plants are better alone; others need to be bunched together. When selecting plants, consider the degree of difficulty in growing them.

The view of the plan should be from the front and above. This helps you to gauge distances between each item and evaluate their relationships from front to back in the tank. Include in your calculations a sufficient quantity of gravel and choice of rocks.

It is better to screen the back of the tank if it is sited against a wall. This hides wires and equipment that would otherwise spoil the view. The screening can be done by painting or spraying the outside back panel pale blue or green. A variety of murals can be purchased as well. These are simply stuck onto the glass. Select a scene appropriate to the overall vista you are planning. Another alternative is to paste cork onto the back panel. This creates a terrific effect in a well-planted aquarium. One last method is to use frosted glass to cover the real wall. Some hobbyists screen off one or both side panels as well. This gives them more control over the amount of light entering the tank.

GRAVEL

The most popular substrate is gravel, which comes in a wide assortment of colors and sizes. The most reliable source of suitable gravel is your local pet store. Gravel from other sources is apt to be contaminated with

A beautiful Red Ryukin Goldfish.

41

unwanted chemicals.

The gravel is the first item placed into the aquarium (unless you have an undergravel filter). All gravel needs to be washed before being set in the tank. Clean small amounts at a time by immersing them in boiling water. Stir well. Run cold water through the gravel until the water is clear. This cleansing should remove dust and undesirable life forms.

Choose gravel that is 2–3 mm (0.08-0.1 in) in size. It should be of a natural color. Brightly colored gravels do not enhance the average planted aquarium. They detract from the scene by drawing the viewer's attention. Furthermore, the dye may leach out and disturb the water condition.

Commercially produced baked clay gravels are often available. They encourage plant growth, provide good surface area for aerobic bacteria, and are often impregnated with fertilizers.

It is a good idea to slope the substrate up from the front to the back of the tank rather than to have an even thickness of gravel over the entire base. The unevenness of the gravel encourages the fish to swim in the front of the tank. Additionally, food and debris accumulate in the front and thus can be more easily siphoned off.

The depth of the gravel at the front of the tank should be about 3.8 cm (1½ in). If you want really good plant growth, place peat and aquarium fertilizers between layers of gravel. The top layer of gravel must be deep enough to withstand the foraging action of the fish.

Retaining rocks or terraces can be constructed so that the water currents do not level the slopes. To avoid symmetry in the aquascaping, the terrace wall should be irregular, not straight. Stones and wood can be strategically placed.

ROCKS

Rocks should be washed, like the gravel, or steam-cleaned to remove harmful materials. Avoid limestone, chalk, marble, and similar calcareous rocks. They have a high calcium content which makes the water hard. Likewise, stay away from soft, crumbly rock. This will also change the mineral content of the water. The best rocks are granite, slate and water-worn sandstone. Do not introduce any rocks with sharp edges that may damage your fish.

Artificial rocks can be used as well to create natural-looking rock scenes. Whether you choose natural or artificial rocks, the colors should blend with the setting.

WOOD

Bogwood and driftwood look attractive in aquariums. Be sure to leach them of unwanted chemicals. Simply immerse the wood in boiling water, then let it dry out thoroughly. Repeat the process several times. Holes cut in logs make nice planting positions. Artificial wood sometimes has a built-in facility for small potted plants.

The wood can be secured by rocks, or it can be bonded to a piece of plastic or glass. The plastic or glass rests on the bottom of the tank and is held in place by the gravel.

THERMOMETER

Be sure to purchase and set up a thermometer, because it is an important aid in monitoring the water temperature. The thermometer may float in the tank or it may fit externally to the glass.

FILTER AND AIRSTONE

The filter and airstone can be installed once the gravel

The translation of the Japanese name is 'brown fish with a bramble head.' Actually the fish is a Copper Oranda.

and rocks are in place. The siphon tube should be just above the gravel level; it is most effective here. The return water spray bar of the single return tube can be fitted to its position just above the planned water surface. Depending on the type, the filter unit can be sited close to or in the aquarium.

Now the water can be added. To minimize disturbance to the gravel, place a saucer or jar in the tank. Pour the water into the jar or dish and let it overflow.

Fill the tank to about one-third of its capacity. Now the plants can be situated. It is better to introduce them when some water is in the tank than when the tank is empty. This way the leaves can float instead of falling on the gravel. Once everything is to your satisfaction, fill the rest of the tank.

The filter can be primed when the tank is full. The airstone can also be put into operation. Check that there are no air bubbles in the filter system pipes.

STOCKING THE AQUARIUM

Fish must not be added for at least 14 days after setting up. The water undergoes a lot of change in the first few weeks ("the new tank syndrome") and needs time to mature. The ammonia levels rise and then level out. The pH and hardness may fluctuate widely. Plants need time to put down roots and anchor themselves to the substrate.

The nitrogen cycle can be hastened by adding a few pieces of raw meat or fish to the tank. Their decomposition encourages aerobic bacterial action.

During this maturation period, you can purchase fish. They can undergo their quarantine at this time. Quarantine is often overlooked by fish owners. Fish are introduced to tanks along with their transport water. This situation poses many risks because the fish or its water may be carrying disease. In addition, the fish is stressed because it is not given time to adapt to the changed water conditions. Remember, the water in two tanks is never identical.

Check the water condition after two weeks. Only when the pH and hardness levels are acceptable can the fish be released.

Plants

Plants not only enhance the aquascene, they are beneficial to both the water and the fish. Plants create oxygen by photosynthesis and they absorb nitrates and other harmful chemicals in the water. They also are food for the goldfish, and they provide shade, hiding areas, and egglaying sites. Plants are esthetically pleasing and make the tank a more natural environment for the fish.

The range of plants available to the coldwater aquarist is considerable. Even some plants that prefer tropical waters can survive in an unheated tank.

This rare specimen has two fixed, recognizable abnormalities. It is a Pompon and an Outturned Operculum. This fish has been developed in China.

You may have heard that plants cannot be kept in a goldfish tank because the fish will uproot, destroy, and eat them. Although the goldfish will forage among the plants, the plants can survive if there is a proper balance between the plants and the fish. In some ways,

the test of a successful aquarist is measured by how well the plants, rather than the fish, are doing. This is because, in many circumstances, the plants require more consideration than the fish.

ALGAE

The one plant no fishkeeper has problems growing is algae. In fact, it cannot be prevented from growing in an aquarium. Rather, it is a matter of keeping the algae in check.

Algae is the simplest form of plant life. It forms one of four divisions within the subkingdom Thallophyta. (Fungi, bacteria, and lichens are the other three divisions.)

Seaweed is probably the best known algae, but there are many smaller species of algae. Some are visible only when in large colonies. They either cloud the water or cover rocks and plants with a green or bluish-brown film. Other types of algae are free-swimming.

Algae reproduces by simple cell division. The daughter cells continue to multiply to rapidly build up colonies when the water is suitable. When conditions are unfavorable, spores are formed. These spores can survive for years. They are present in the atmosphere because they are carried by the wind.

The controlling factor of green algae is sunlight and, to a lesser extent, artificial light. The light enables the algae to grow and reproduce. If the light is restricted, the algae cannot flourish. For example, a pond quickly turns green on a sunny day. However, if higher plant life deprives the algae of light, the algae cannot prosper. Only if there is light in excess of the needs of the higher forms of plant life can the algae grow. Hence, regulation of light is important in an aquarium. The more the plants flourish, the less algae is a problem if the light is sufficient but not excessive. Bear in mind, however, that brown algae reproduces when conditions lack light. Therefore, the correct amount of light can be determined only on an individual tank basis.

A controlled amount of algae is beneficial for a tank, both from a decorative standpoint and from a nutritional aspect. Goldfish eat algae, which has minute animal life growing on it. If an excess of algae builds up on the aquarium glass, simply scrape it away and adjust the lighting accordingly.

SELECTION

Aquatic plants exhibit many types of leaf shape. Clearly the shapes and colors appeal to people on an individual basis. Suitable plants for an aquarium are of two basic types: free-floating and those with roots to anchor the plants. Aquatic plants draw most of their nutrients directly through their leaves and stems rather than through the root system.

Some plants are best given an area of free space around them. These are specimen plants. Other plants should be planted in groups to form dense foliage at the sides and back of the aquarium. Low-growing plants are better suited to the foreground. Plants that grow to the water surface should be planted at the back. Here they will not impair the view yet will hide unsightly tubes and pumps.

CUTTINGS

The majority of plants offered for sale are in the form of cuttings taken from other plants. A cutting may be the top growing shoot, the middle section of a plant, or it may be the lower area complete with roots. Each of these cuttings is fine.

Only the roots need to regrow in the case of the top cutting. The shoot can be planted in a small pot with some growing medium. Root hormone compounds can be added to encourage rapid growth.

The middle cutting needs both roots and side branches to develop. The end result is a bushier plant because there is typically more than one growing leaf bud. Base cuttings also become fuller plants for the same reason.

Once a plant is established, trim the top cuttings, or the top and middle, to build up the number of plants in the aquarium. As a beginning plant grower, limit the number of species. Concentrate on a few varieties to fully understand their habits. By making notes of the preferred temperatures, locations and tank mates, you can decide for yourself what plants are best suited to your aquarium. Comments in books are necessarily of a general nature.

STOLONS AND RHIZOMES

Many plants grow by sending out runners or stolons. These are modified stems which may grow under or above the substrate. After a short length of growth, the stolons sport stems and roots. Once established, they break away from the mother plants to repeat the process. These young growths can be detached prematurely to be planted in another area of the tank. It is advisable to let them produce stems and roots before transplanting them.

Rhizomes are swollen adventitious stems. They swell in order to store food so that the plant can grow from one year to the next. Rhizomes can be propagated by cutting them when new shoots appear. The rhizome will regrow.

Reproduction of aquarium plants is vegetative, so it is relatively simple. Sexual reproduction can occur as well. Rarely, though, do conditions in an aquarium contribute to the surface flowering of sexual reproduction.

PLANTING

Plants may be pushed carefully into the substrate. Their shoots can be covered with gravel. If there are no shoots, the plants can then be tied together and weighted with ceramic weights. Even better is to place them in small pots or available from most aquatic or pet supply stores. No matter how good the source, however, each plant should be carefully inspected for

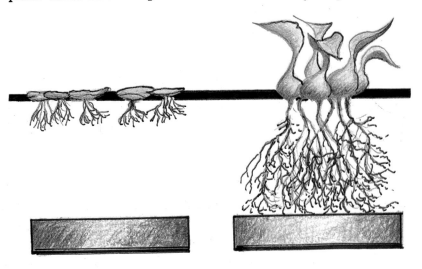

bags which can be hidden by rocks. The pots can then be covered with large gravel to prevent foraging by the fish.

Inspect the plants regularly for signs of poor condition. Remove dead leaves and do not allow a plant to grow too large for the tank. Be sure that floating plants do not take over the water surface. They can shade out too much light and reduce the exchange of oxygen at the surface.

POPULAR PLANTS

The following plants are signs of parasites and their eggs. Wash all plants in clean running water. Remove any dead or dying leaves.

Dwarf Rush or Sedge
Acorus   gramineus
SIZE: 8–45 cm (3–18 in)
pH: neutral to slightly acid, 6.8–7
LIGHTING: normal
TEMPERATURE: 15–20°C (59–68°F)
HARDNESS: slightly soft
REPRODUCTION: cut the rhizome
GENERALLY: An attractive plant with long ribbon-like leaves. The dwarf variety, *A.*

g. pussilus, is ideal for foreground planting. A slow-growing but hardy plant.

Hygrophila
Alternanthera   spp
SIZE: 50 cm (20 in)
pH: neutral
LIGHTING: bright to intense
TEMPERATURE: 16–20°C (60–68°F)
HARDNESS: slight
REPRODUCTION: cuttings
GENERALLY: Unusual because of their pink to deep red leaves. A drawback is the level of required illumination. They are not the easiest plants to establish.

Laceleaf Plant
Aponogeton madagascariensis
SIZE: 15–20 cm (6–8 in)
pH: 6-8
LIGHTING: normal and diffused
TEMPERATURE: 16–20°C (60–68°F)
HARDNESS: moderately hard
REPRODUCTION: cuttings
GENERALLY: A good plant for middle and rear tank positions. Plant a few together for the best effect. Handle with care because the stems are brittle.

Fanwort
Cabomba   spp
SIZE: over 90 cm (36 in)
pH: slightly acid, 6.5–7
LIGHTING: bright

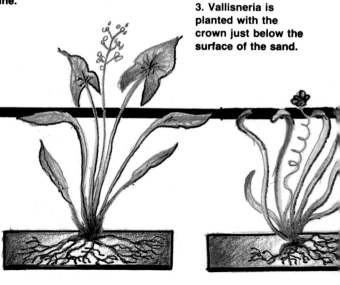

1. Laceplants and Swordplants are planted with their crowns just above the gravel line.

2. Arrowheads are planted with their crowns at the gravel line.

3. Vallisneria is planted with the crown just below the surface of the sand.

TEMPERATURE: 13–25°C (55–77°F)
HARDNESS: soft
REPRODUCTION: top cuttings of at least 15 cm (6 in)
GENERALLY: Tall, deep green plants suitable for the back or sides of the aquarium. They require loam substrate and regular pruning.

Chinese or Japanese Cress
Cardamine   lytra
SIZE: 25–38 cm (10–15 in)
pH: neutral to slightly acid
LIGHTING: bright
TEMPERATURE: 14–22° C (57–71°F)
HARDNESS: moderately soft
REPRODUCTION: cuttings
GENERALLY: A plant that is easy to grow. It has small, variably shaped, pale green leaves. It is best suited to the middle or back of the tank. It retains its color better in colder water.

Callitriche   **spp**
SIZE: 10–100 cm (4–40 in)
pH: neutral
LIGHTING: very strong
TEMPERATURE: 5–15°C (41–59°F)
HARDNESS: soft
REPRODUCTION: cuttings
GENERALLY: These plants have small linear to ovate leaves which grow from thread-like stems. Good oxygenators which grow quickly.

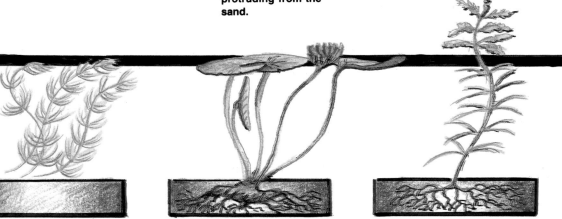

4. Cabomba and Ceratophyllum are planted in bunches or allowed to float.

5. Water lilies come from tubers which must be planted with the vegetating tip just protruding from the sand.

6. Almost any aquatic plant can be simply thrust into the sand where it will root.

Hornwort *Ceratophyllum demersum*
SIZE: 45 cm (18 in)
pH: neutral
LIGHTING: bright
TEMPERATURE: 5–18°C (41–65°F)
HARDNESS: moderately hard
REPRODUCTION: cuttings
GENERALLY: Popular in aquaculture. The narrow leaves have one or two forks which grow from branched stems. Attractive but brittle.

Sword Plant
Echinodorus cordifolius
SIZE: up to 60 cm (24 in)
pH: neutral
LIGHTING: bright
TEMPERATURE: 10–27°C (50–81°F)
HARDNESS: moderately hard
REPRODUCTION: division of plantlets from main shoot
GENERALLY: An impressive plant with large, ovate leaves in bright green. A peat substrate is preferred.

Pondweed
***Egeria and Elodea* sp**
SIZE: over 2 m (2 ft)
pH: slightly alkaline, 7–8
LIGHTING: bright
TEMPERATURE: 5–20°C (41–68°F)
HARDNESS: moderate to moderately hard
REPRODUCTION: cuttings
GENERALLY: *Egria densa* and *Elodea canadensis* are favorites for coldwater ponds and aquariums. The long, narrow stems sport linear leaves in whorls. Ideal for backgrounds. The fast-growing leaves need regular pruning.

Spike Bush or Hairgrass
Eleocharis acicularis
SIZE: up to 30 cm (12 in)
pH: slightly acid, 6.5–7
LIGHTING: normal to bright
TEMPERATURE: 10–25°C (50–77°F)
HARDNESS: moderately hard
REPRODUCTION: runners detached from main stolon
GENERALLY: A simple yet effective plant. It forms stands of grass-like tufts that are well suited to foregrounds and near rocks. The leaves are tiny on long, thin stems. A substrate containing loam provides good anchorage.

***Ludwigia* spp**
SIZE: up to 45 cm (18 in)
pH: neutral
LIGHTING: bright
TEMPERATURE: 15–25°C (59–77°F)
HARDNESS: not critical, 110–190 ppm
REPRODUCTION: cuttings
GENERALLY: Best planted in bunches in the middle or rear of the tank. These tall,

slim-branched plants bear small, elliptical, paired leaves. They are light green to yellow in color.

Water milfoil
Myriophyllum **spp**
SIZE: over 120 cm (48 in)
pH: variable according to species
LIGHTING: bright
TEMPERATURE: up to 25°C (77°F)
HARDNESS: variable according to species
REPRODUCTION: cuttings; remove lower leaves or cut the rhizome
GENERALLY: These plants sport fine, fern-like whorls on an erect stem. The plants may be rooted or free-floating.

Spatterdock, Cow Lily
Nuphar **spp**
SIZE: 10–30 cm (4–12 in) leaves
pH: alkaline
LIGHTING: bright
TEMPERATURE: up to 25°C (77°F)
HARDNESS: not critical
REPRODUCTION: cut the stout rhizome
GENERALLY: Suited to the larger aquarium.

Arrowhead
Sagittaria **spp**
SIZE: up to 90 cm (36 in)
pH: slightly alkaline
LIGHTING: normal to weak
TEMPERATURE: up to 25°C (77°F)
HARDNESS: moderately hard
REPRODUCTION: runners, cut the stolon
GENERALLY: Hardy plants

German Veiltails.

The Oranda is a lionhead type with a dorsal fin. The Japanese sometimes call it Oranda Shishigashira.

with long, linear leaves. Best in bunches at the mid-regions of the aquarium.

Vallisneria spiralis
SIZE: up to 60 cm (24 in)
pH: neutral
LIGHTING: bright
TEMPERATURE: 15-22°C (59–72°F)

HARDNESS: moderately soft to hard
REPRODUCTION: runners, cut the stolon
GENERALLY: Another popular aquatic plant. It has long, narrow, ribbon-like leaves.

Varieties of Goldfish

There are over 100 varieties of goldfish. However, many forms are not seen outside of China and Japan. This book will discuss some popular varieties available to the average enthusiast. In some instances, you may need to contact a goldfish specialist or society to locate a supplier.

Beginners are strongly advised to restrict their interests to the most popular varieties. These specimens are hardy, breed well and do not require special treatment. More delicate varieties can be kept once experience is gained.

SELECTING

Study each specimen carefully for any signs of poor health or damage to the body and fins. Your fish should swim with no problem, have a clean body and fins, and be free of abrasions and parasites. Choose a fish with good color. Avoid specimens with faded markings and a variable reflection to the scales. If any fish in the tank of your selection seems unfit, pass over that one. Any other fish from the same aquarium may be incubating the illness apparent in its tankmate.

Upon completion of your choice and purchase, your fish will probably be placed in a plastic bag containing some of the tank water. Once home, float the bag in your tank for at least ten minutes to allow the temperatures to equate. Open the bag and gently let the fish swim free. Never drop a fish into the water.

The Common Goldfish is still the most popular variety. It is an excellent choice because it has many virtues and no drawbacks. The fish is well proportioned and ideally suited to a pond or aquarium. The best examples are of metallic type. The most favored colors are red-orange or yellow. Self-colored with fins trimmed in black are also attractive.

The Wakin is the common goldfish of Japan, though it is of Chinese origin. It is similar to the Western version, but it has a double caudal or tailfin. Deep red is the preferred color.

The Jikin is commonly known as the Butterfly Tail.

Goldfish have been bred to be observed from above. This gorgeous specimen is a Tancho Ryukin-type. The Tancho is the Japanese crane with a red spot on its head. Certain color varieties of koi are also called Tancho.

It is believed to have been bred from the Wakin. The caudal fin, when viewed from the rear, has a characteristic X shape. The two upper halves of the tail are almost perpendicular, while the lower halves are about 45 degrees to the body axis.

The London Shubunkin is a color, rather than an anatomical, variation of the Common Goldfish. It lacks the metallic shine and is often called a Calico. A good example has a steel-blue background on which are red, yellow, black, brown, and violet patches.

The Bristol Shubunkin is a hardy and handsome fish with well-developed fins. The caudal fin is large, well forked, and has rounded lobes. The fin should be carried erect.

The Comet is a graceful and fast-swimming fish. The body depth should not be more than one-third the body length. The elongated caudal fin may be about three-quarters as long as the body. The caudal tail spines should run horizontally for at least half their length. The other fins are enlarged when compared to the Common Goldfish, with a gentle curve to their outline. Red and yellow are common colors, but silver and red are also available. The scales are of the metallic type.

The Tancho Singletail is a variety of the Comet. The caudal tail is less deeply forked. The color is silver with a red cap. The fins are white. Often the fins or the body exhibit traces of pink.

The Fantail is the Western version of the Ryukin. Its body is eggshaped. The anal and caudal fins are paired.

The dorsal fin is large, about half the body height or more. The caudal fins are large, rounded and moderately forked. They must be carried erect. This fish is available in both metallic and nacreous types. It comes in a range of colors, from selfs to calicos.

The Ryukin is the second most popular variety in Japan. It is the original version of the Fantail. Both varieties are much the same in body shape. However, the Ryukin differs from the Fantail in that it has a distinct hump to its back, just behind the head. Its fins are somewhat more flowing as well. Both the Ryukin and the Fantail have a telescope-eyed form.

The Tosakin is more readily known as the Peacock Tail. It is believed to have been developed from the Ryukin. Selective breeding has resulted in a characteristic tail which, when viewed from above, fans like a peacock's tail. The lower lobes fold over to point toward the head. This fish is a poor swimmer. Exhibition stock must have long ventral and pectoral fins. The anal fin must be

paired and about half the length of the caudal fin.

The Telescope-eyed Goldfish has eyes extending from the head on appendages. The extent of telescoping varies, and it is possible for one eye to be normal and one telescoped. The eyesight of this variety is not good, and the eyes can be damaged easily. The body

Celestial goldfish always have their eyes pointed to the heavens.

shape resembles that of the Ryukin. The reflective type may be metallic or nacreous. Many colors are available. It is not recommended for community tanks or for garden ponds.

The Veiltail has greatly enlarged fins which flow as the fish moves. The body is a deep eggshape. The dorsal fin is high. It should be as tall as the body is deep. The caudal fin is long, flowing, and paired. The lower edges should be squared. The Veiltail fish may be of the metallic or nacreous type. This variety can be found with telescope eyes. It is not well suited to outdoor life.

The Moor is an all-black variation of the Telescope-eyed Veiltail. The standard of excellence of this variety is probably the highest of any goldfish type. In many specimens, the black gives rise to a brassy coloration as the fish ages. The telescope eyes are not apparent in young fish. They become obvious as the fish gets older. This fish is of the metallic type. It is not recommended for an outdoor pond.

The Lionhead was developed in Japan from the earlier Chinese type known as the Maruko. This fish has short fins and the warty head growth. The dorsal fin is absent altogether. The anal fins are paired and the caudal fin doubled. The Lionhead is a metallic type, but there is also a nacreous form.

The Oranda was developed by crossing the Lionhead with the Veiltail. The head has raspberry-like growth on it. This feature is called the hood in Western countries and the wen in Japan. The warty growth should cover the entire head and be evenly distributed. The Oranda is of the metallic type, although nacreous variants are available.

The Pearlscale is noted for its unusual scales. These are raised in the center and of a lighter color. This pattern creates a pearl-like sheen. The body and fins are similar to the Fantail. The caudal fin is less forked, however, than that of the Fantail. The Pearlscale often has a pronounced droop to its abdomen. Both metallic and nacreous types are available.

The Pompon has fleshy growths between the nostrils. These can be extensive, even grotesque. Such a modification is susceptible to damage and disease. This fish is similar to the Lionhead in its overall shape. It may or may not have a dorsal fin.

The Celestial has eyes which stare upwards. This is because they are positioned on the top, rather than the ends, of outgrowths of the head. No dorsal fin is present. The other fins resemble those of the Ryukin.

The Bubble-eye has liquid-

Three commercial quality Shubunkins.

filled sacs or bladders growing from beneath the eyes. They are easily damaged but can repair themselves. This fish comes in both metallic and nacreous forms.

The Meteor is an eggshaped fish. The tail or caudal fin is absent. The other fins are enlarged in order to compensate. The Meteor does move about, but with reduced mobility.

A small-scale breeder could probably dispose of his fish in the local pet stores. The goal of the average breeder should be to breed for the needs of the general pet market rather than to exhibition standards. The price and quality must be reasonably comparable to that of commercial breeders. Since competition is fierce on the commercial level, prices are kept at a low level.

This Water Bubble-eye's head is so heavy it must rest on the bottom of the tank most of the time.

Breeding

Breeding is an interesting aspect of the goldfish hobby. Careful thought and preparation is required, however, because a lot of work is involved.

It is unlikely that any returns from fish sold will cover the overhead.

EXHIBITION GOLDFISH

If you plan to exhibit goldfish, then purchase superb initial stock. Do not buy pet-quality fish in an attempt to upgrade them through selective breeding. Such a process is time-consuming, costly, and impractical. Additionally, if your initial stock is substandard, no amount of breeding will produce good quality. It is better to pay a high price early on to a breeder whose fish have show potential. This way you gain the benefit of that breeder's years of hard work and experience in building up his line of goldfish.

SELECTION

Breeding is all about selecting the best fish and retaining them for further breeding. The idea is to steadily improve the overall standard of your stock. Purchase young breeding adults rather than immature fish. The quality of an immature fish remains to be seen. The best age at which to breed a female is at full maturity, about two years of age. A male may be bred any time after one year of age.

Note the strong and weak points of a fish. You may select a fish for a particular feature, such as color, body shape, caudal fin shape, etc.

Champion Japanese Ryukin.

Or you may be interested in the overall quality of a fish. However you choose, breeding health and vigor are always important criteria.

Choose a popular and hardy variety. Learn all you can about that variety before breeding others.

INHERITANCE

All features are passed from one generation to the next by units of coded information known as genes.

Champion Jikin.

Fifty percent of an offspring's genes are inherited from one parent and fifty percent from the other. Genes, as well as the environment, determine the quality of a fish. A fish may have superior genes, but its full potential cannot be developed if the husbandry is poor.

Given the impact of heredity, it is important to know the breeding history of each fish. It is a sound idea to keep detailed breeding records on each fish. The more you know about a fish's line of descent, the better you can estimate its suitability for breeding. Once you have an established stock, do not introduce a fish of unknown origin. The fish may look good, but it may carry genes that would be detrimental to your stock.

SEXING

Most egglayers, such as goldfish, are difficult to sex. The sexes are similar, or sexually non-dimorphic. Only at breeding time are the sexes distinguishable. A female in breeding condition shows an abdominal swelling as the eggs form within her. A male exhibits white spots, or tubercles, on his gill plates.

THE EGGS

Goldfish are oviparous, which means they lay eggs. They do not give birth to live young. Goldfish do not bury their eggs. They randomly scatter them. A female will shed thousands of eggs as the male releases millions of sperm in a cloudy white milt.

In the wild, many eggs remain unfertilized or are eaten by bacteria and fish. The remaining eggs adhere to plants and other surfaces. They hatch in comparative safety, away from their parents who would devour them. (Goldfish do not display parental interest in their offspring.)

The rate at which the eggs hatch depends on the water temperature. The higher the temperature, the more quickly the eggs hatch. Temperature, space, and the availability of food control the growth of the fry (newly hatched fish).

BREEDING TANKS

It is possible to breed goldfish in the display tank. However, this is not productive. Most of the eggs would be consumed quickly by the parents and other fish. Furthermore, you want control over which fish mate. Pairings cannot be controlled in a display tank. Therefore, isolate the chosen pair in a spawning tank.

The breeding tank should be about 60 by 38 by 30 cm deep (25 by 15 by 12 in). The water conditions should be similar to those of the main tank. The temperature should be about 18°C (64.5°F).

Include one or two plants or spawning mops, a simple and non-powerful filter, and an airstone. Some fine netting can be suspended deep in the water. As the eggs are shed, they will pass through the net to settle on the aquarium base. The fine netting will prevent the parents from gaining access to the eggs.

MATING

As the weather warms in late spring, the breeding season commences. The breeding pair can be placed into the spawning tank. Some breeders separate the fish with a glass division for 24 hours. Some place the male in the tank first, then put the female in one day later.

Once together, the male should chase the female around the aquarium for long periods of time. Between each chase is a short rest period. Eventually the female settles and the male swims alongside her. The pair vibrate their bodies; and the female releases her eggs and the male his milt. This process is repeated until the female has shed all her eggs. There may be some damage to the fins or scales after mating is complete.

If the mating is not complete in 24 hours, leave the pair together for a few days. Feed them livefoods, such as earthworms or daphnia. If no spawning occurs after seven days, split the pair up. Reintroduce them a few days later or change one of the partners.

Once spawning is complete, remove the parents. Reduce the water level to 15 cm (6 in). The reduction in depth assures an adequate oxygen supply. Increase the temperature by 2–3°C. This will encourage the eggs to hatch in five days.

REARING THE FRY

The newly hatched fry are about 6 mm (¼″) large. Provide illumination at all times for the best development. The fry will survive their first 48 hours of life by eating the remains of their yolk sacs. After this, they need frequent meals. Both liquid and powder fry foods can be purchased.

Alternatively, you can prepare fry food, infusoria or brine shrimp, yourself. Infusoria are microscopic, unicellular organisms cultured by boiling some water. After the water cools, place it into large jars with some bruised lettuce, a banana skin or some other vegetation. Place the jar in a warm, darkened area for seven days. The water will be cloudy and have an unpleasant smell. The infusoria can be siphoned off and fed to the fry.

Brine shrimp are tiny crustaceans. Cultures are prepared by adding one teaspoon of marine or cooking salt to a liter of water. Add about one teaspoon of brine shrimp eggs purchased from your pet dealer. The water must

be well aerated and kept at a temperature around 25°C (77°F). The eggs should hatch in about 24 hours.

The fry can tackle larger foods once they are 14 days old. Foods such as crushed goldfish flakes, minced egg yolks, earthworms, and other livefoods can be offered.

The water level in the tank can be raised a little each day. Be sure the added water

In most random breedings of goldfish, the young come out looking like they are hardly related to each other. If you are going to breed goldfish, breed from the best parents available.

is clean and heated to the correct temperature. Change 25% of the water content each week.

CULLING

It is better to rear fewer but better goldfish than to raise fish in great numbers. Hence, you should continually assess the fry as they grow. Remove any that are deformed or of poor quality.

The fry can be inspected by gathering them in a small sieve (do not use a net) when they are 14 days old. Place them in a bowl. You can evaluate them with the aid of a hand lens.

Unwanted fry can be placed into the main tank to be eaten by the adult fish, or they can be placed in a bowl of ice cubes. Culling may seem cruel, but you are only doing what would happen in nature—allowing only the fittest to survive.

Photos by
Dr. Herbert R.
Axelrod, David
Axelrod, Burkhard
Kahl, Midori Shobo,
Barry Pengilley, and
Fred Rosenzweig.

GOLDFISH AS A NEW PET

has been written by one the world's leading pet authorities. The author gives all the necessary practical guidance for the beginner to meet his everyday needs. Meaningful color illustrations assist the beginner in identifying various color and fin varieties of goldfish with information on keeping them happy and healthy. Special chapters deal with aerating and filtering the water, growing plants and aquascaping, as well as the varieties of goldfish and how to breed them.

This book is published by the *TROPICAL FISH HOBBYIST* magazine, the world's largest aquarium magazine. We are totally dedicated to the proper education of beginning aquarists . . . your future is our future.

T.F.H. Publications, Inc., ● TFH Plaza ● Neptune City, NJ 07753

This book is completely manufactured in the USA.   U.S. $6.95/CAN $9.95

ISBN 0-86622-606-0